ACKNOWL

I need to shout at a
helped me tremendo
life, and who continue to help me every
single day.

1. My Heavenly Father

2. My Family
Soneil Charles (father)
Maunda Charles (mother)
Sonayah Charles (older sister)
Jael Charles (older sister)
Adanya Charles (younger sister)
Caleb Charles (younger brother)

3. My Church
Spirit of Faith Christian Center

4. My Four Best Friends
Kennedy Adams (best friend)
Asia Lee (bestie)
Micah Wilson (bestfrann)
Jeremey Wooten (bestieee)
(And yes, I have four best friends and what about it, LOL. I love them all equally.)

5. Myself 😊

All of these people have contributed to my deliverance in different ways that I'm very grateful for and appreciate tremendously.

Thank you, all of you! I love you all very much and couldn't ask for a better support system!

Written by Nailah Charles
Illustrated by Jael Charles

Copyright © 2021 by **Nailah Charles**

All rights reserved. No part of this publication may be reproduced, distributed, or transmitted in any form or by any means, without prior written permission.

PurposefulTime, LLC
Silver Spring, MD
www.purposefultime.com

Delivered / Nailah Charles. -- 1st ed.
ISBN 978-0-578-87030-4

AUTHOR'S NOTE

Hey! I'm glad that you've decided to read my book. That means a lot to me. 😊 I have a few things to tell you before you dive in.

1. I wrote this book because Holy Spirit told me to. Writing this book wasn't my own idea.
2. I wrote this book because my story is worth being known.
3. I wrote this book at the age of 16 in the middle the COVID-19 pandemic in 2020.
4. This book has a lot of quality information that you or somebody you know can use.
5. I kinda rant in this book a little bit, so if you wanna hear the tea, READ THE WHOLE THING LOL! 😊
6. Parts of this book are written in text message form, hence the title 'Delivered'. It is designed to be relatable, easy to read, and understandable for teens and even pre-teens.

Please enjoy :)

TABLE OF CONTENTS

My Home Page - Intro............................ 1

Not Sexting, Sexual Assault............... 17

Low Battery – The Pitch-Black Phase
.... 57

Everyone's Fav 6-letter word...School
.... 101

#NoCap - Relationships......................123

No Filter – Insecurities & Self-
Confidence..139

My Messages - DELIVERED 161

"If you want a rainbow, sometimes you have to put up with the rain."

1
Add Number

1	2 ABC	3 DEF
4 GHI	5 JKL	6 MNO
7 PQRS	8 TUV	9 WXYZ
*	0 +	#

 Favorites Recents Contacts **Keypad** Voicemail

CHAPTER 1

My Home Page - Intro

We all have different perspectives on life, especially while we are young, still growing, and maturing. A lot of times, all we see and all we go through becomes our biggest picture. We get caught up in things we shouldn't or even things we should, and it shapes us to be the person we are growing into. Life has become this roller coaster for me mentally, emotionally, spiritually, and even physically. I've lost focus on things that are very important to me. I've compromised my emotional stability for others to have the best, not realizing that it was slowly decreasing my ability to view myself as valuable, worth it, beautiful, smart and so much more. I've looked at other people and have become torn to the fact that I've risked a lot for them, and they don't even know it. So, I've contemplated whether it was a mistake or not because I have this huge heart for people, especially the ones I care about. I have this heart that pulls me to make a huge effort to make their days better and to make sure they are happy before I am. It's almost like my heart is married to people who I didn't even get engaged to, if that makes any sense...LOL. I've lost myself when I thought I was just really starting to find myself. Which was becoming very tormenting to me.

Looking in the wrong places for satisfaction, attraction and approval is draining and useless. I've been through so much in my 16 years of living so far. A lot of what I've been through has been behind closed doors and has never really been shared with even some of the closest people to me.

When I was younger, I thought I knew so much about life, in general. I clouded my mind with my thoughts, which led me to places that I didn't want to be at all. So, I decided to write this book about life, my life, in particular. A teenager living in a world full of toxicity, artificial relationships, emotional attachments, suicidal thoughts, sexual assault, failing in school and lots more. Yes, I'm writing this book as a teenager, and yes, I'm still learning about life and the people around me. So no, I don't have it all put together, and maybe I will never have it all put together, but I know someone who is all knowing and someone who will prevail when all else fails.

So, before we begin these deep, heart-felt, emotional, amazing, eye-opening stories/rants, I ask that when you are reading this you are open-minded and take advantage of the quality information being shared, and apply it to your life, so that you can better yourself.

God has a plan for each and every one of his children. So, stop comparing your growth and success to someone else's, because at the end of the day God knows you better than anyone else. and he knows what you can handle in each season of your life. Take it from me and trust God. I guarantee that after you finish reading this book your perspective on life will change.

I am going to be sharing five topics with you by taking you through my life. You will learn about my experiences and all the ups and downs of my 16 years of living so far. I can tell you right now, I am going to mention God, Jesus, church and my relationship with Jesus and Holy Spirit A LOT. So, if you feel uncomfortable with any of those topics, keep reading. Keep reading because being comfortable is the enemy to growth. In other words, growth comes from you being uncomfortable. Keep reading because you obviously picked up this book for a reason. Keep reading because God is trying to speak to you, through me, and He has been trying to speak to you, but you don't think He knows or understands what you are going through. Let me tell you that He not only knows, He sees what you are going through, and He understands. He has been trying to help you, but you keep shutting Him out. So, keep reading.

Life can be full of opportunities and distractions, but you have to choose which road you are going to take. You also have to choose who you take on your journey with you because everybody in your life isn't intended to stay. Some people in your life are only there for a period and some will be there forever...maybe. Life can be as hard or as easy as you make it, if you are willing to change it. Maya Angelou once said that,

"You will face many defeats in life, but never let yourself be defeated."

This is going to be a crazy ride so grab some popcorn, a drink and most importantly, a pen to take notes on the notes pages provided at the end of each chapter. You are going to want to strap in and lock in because you are about to learn the crazy story behind my beautiful, dimpled face.🥲 You are about to see how everything that came to destroy me in my first sixteen years of living, I destroyed 💪, because I'm 'Delivered". Welcome to my story.

DELIVERED · 13

14 · NAILAH CHARLES

"Strength isn't always shown in what you can hold on to, sometimes it's shown in what you can let go of."

- Drake

2

Add Number

1	2 ABC	3 DEF
4 GHI	5 JKL	6 MNO
7 PQRS	8 TUV	9 WXYZ
*	0 +	#

Favorites

Recents

Contacts

Keypad

Voicemail

CHAPTER 2

Not Sexting, Sexual Assault

I was sexually assaulted twice in the second grade. At the time I didn't know it was sexual assault, because who was learning and thinking about that in the second grade.? Not me. I just knew it wasn't right at all. I was very reserved, especially in elementary through middle school. In the second grade, I was just starting to learn my multiplication tables. My sexual assault story isn't as extreme as other people's, but it was severe to me. Once again, I didn't think I would go through something like this. At the time, I didn't understand what it was and how it was going to affect me in the long run. It all came so fast. Sexual assault is not something that you should take lightly or play around with. You never know if someone you are really close to has been through sexual assault or sexual harassment. You really have to be sensitive to people's feelings when it comes to this topic. This is the first time I'm really opening up to the world about this. I felt as if I did it earlier in my life people wouldn't believe me.

I was so mad at what happened to me. 'Til this day, I have a hard time hugging people for long periods or being extra close to people for long periods of time. I just feel like something is going to go wrong, but I know that it's just the devil trying to get into my head and scare me. I have to realize that going through what I went through does not make me disgusting, or less of a person. I am still me. I am still beautiful, and nothing can change that. Although what I went through was very traumatizing for me, I will never let it transform the woman that God called me to be. As I tell you my story, please understand that it may not be extreme to you, but it was very extreme to me at that young age, and it was hard for me to comprehend. Also, be considerate of the fact that I am willing to tell my story to you, so learn something from it that can help you or others.

I had just moved to a new school. Before, I was going to a private Christian school, so everything was new to me now. I didn't have to wear a uniform. I didn't have chapel throughout the week. The new school was dirtier, no offense of course, LOL. It was just different because it was public school and not private school. As the school year went on, I began to get more comfortable with the environment and its people, but never too comfortable to the point where I'd lose myself. I've always been quiet in school. I talked, but not that much, just enough to make some friends and for the teacher to know a little bit about me. I had a nice small, funny and smart friend group. We all got along very well and always encouraged each other in our class.

Assault #1:

I was about seven or eight when it happened. I didn't see it coming at all, and I was very mad that it happened afterwards. At the elementary school I went to, each grade had lunch and recess at different times. For example, if you were in fifth grade, there were usually at least three or four other fifth grade classes, so when it was time for lunch and recess, we would all go together. Anyway, this day two of my guy 'friends' had been fighting all day over me. 'Til this day, I don't know why, because I never ever claimed them or dated anyone before. 🤦🏻‍♀️ Like, we were in second grade, and they were fighting over me. Dumb...

We had just finished our recess period, and at the end of each recess period we would have to line up quietly by class. So, I did as I was told always. I was quiet. I put my toys away that I used for that day and got right in the back of the line. But this day, guy 'friend' #1 challenged guy 'friend' #2 and said to him, "Prove she's yours". So, I'm just standing there like OMG 😲 what are they about to do? Guy 'friend' #2 then says, "Ok, I will." Mind you they were yelling to each other across the blacktop, so a lot of the other fifth graders can hear them, but apparently the teachers weren't paying attention to what was going on at all.

So, then guy 'friend' #2 proceeds to run up to me and kiss my cheek. All I hear is everyone around me going "ouuuu Nailah has a boyfriend!", "Aww he just kissed her!". In my mind I'm like I need to tell my teacher, I need to tell my teacher. Before I go to tell my teacher, I look at guy 'friend' #2 and slap him right in the face in front of everybody. All my classmates are like, "ouuuuuuu." While guy 'friend' #1 is laughing so hard he almost falls onto the blacktop. I am standing there in shock glaring at guy 'friend' #1. I look at him for a few seconds more 😳 and then my small right hand comes out of my coat pocket and slaps him right in the face. I didn't care about how much trouble I was going to get into afterwards. I just was so mad, so I took matters into my own hands...literally and slapped him. 💁🏾‍♀️

    Long story short, don't do what I did and slap someone...LOL. Although, I felt like it needed to be done. In that moment I chose to live by my feelings alone and not confront the Holy Spirit before doing what I did. When we as people decide to live by our feelings and not make smart decisions, we put ourselves at risk to fall into traps of the enemy. When you are a child of God, and have a relationship with God and Holy Spirit, we especially need to constantly keep ourselves in check, because people are always looking for us to break and crack under pressure. We must remain so rooted in the word of God that when something comes up that is supposed to get us off track, we realize it, and we don't let it overtake us.

Assault #2

Again, I was in the second grade when it all happened. In my class we used to have this thing called math rotations. Basically, you would be in a group of two or three other classmates, and you would rotate around the class to all the stations. At each station there were different ways to practice what we were learning in that topic for math. Every time we learned a new topic, we would have math rotations in the days to follow, in order to keep the strategies in our heads. Usually, in my rotation group, I was very rarely grouped up with my friends because we would get off topic a lot.

There was this one time that I was paired up with one of my guy 'friends' from my friend group. We were so excited to be together for the first time ever. I didn't realize that it would be the last time I would be paired up with him ever. Like I mentioned earlier, I wasn't thinking about sexual assault in second grade. I knew what was right and what was wrong, but I didn't realize how wrong it was. So, the station that my 'friend' and I were at when it happened was by our class cubbies. It wasn't in the cubbies, but it was right outside of the cubbies. At that station we were using dice for our activity.

I was really set on the fact that I trusted this boy with my second grade understanding of trust. I never would have thought he would do what he did to me then deny it.

Now, we've been at the rotation station for about 10 minutes. The whole class was on their last rotation, so I knew that we were going to start wrapping up soon. Usually at the end of math rotation it was a little chaotic because everyone was taking their materials back to the bins. My teacher had just said, "Alright class it's time to clean up and get ready for our reading rotations." Everyone in my class knew that once she said that or something close to that we would need to stop what we were doing and clean up our stations.

So, my friend that I am at the station with throws all the dice into the cubbies. I started collecting all the dice from under people's backpacks and jackets. He comes in the cubby area and starts doing the same thing. He collects two and I collect three. We both know that there are six die. We began to look around for the sixth die.

Simultaneously, we both realize that the sixth die was in between my legs, closer to my crotch area. He launches himself at me and tackles me. So, now I am flat on my back trying to get him off of me. At this point, I am starting to get mad because he was doing the most and he was FLAT ON

TOP of me. Like we were literally face-to-face. If anyone of us moved the wrong way, we would have kissed each other. He then proceeds to reach in between my legs and grabs the die. Instead of taking his hand out from between my legs after grabbing the die, he touches my vagina from outside of my pants very, very, very inappropriately. At this point I knew something was wrong.

I use all my strength and push him off of me. I sit up and he runs out of the cubby area. I sit up and think immediately to myself I need to tell my teacher. So, I get myself up trying to hold back all my tears and go to my teacher. I lean over the red rectangular table that she is sitting at, as all of my other classmates are coming up to the other side of the table to put their materials away loudly. And I say in a very, soft voice "(the name of my friend) touched my vagina." She looks at me and says, "What?" So, I repeat what I said the first time. She says ok and tells me to go sit down. As I'm heading back to my seat, she calls my 'friend' and hands him a principal office pass with a sticky note that describes the situation.

Now, my heart is beating because I don't like telling on people, especially my friends, so I felt bad, but I knew I did the right thing. No more than seven minutes passed when the main office secretary came on the intercom and said, "Can I please have Nailah Charles to the office for a moment please?" My teacher responds and says yes, then signals me to go to the office. I walked down the quiet hallways of my school wondering what my principal was going to ask me that wasn't on the sticky note. I reach the main office and the secretary tells me to go to the principal's office. As I am walking to her office and see my 'friend' in the room right before her office. We make eye contact, and I can see that he was mad and that he had been crying.

I open her office door and she instructs me to take a seat. I sit down and she asks me to tell her exactly what happened. I tell her and then she says, "You know this is not something to play with, right?" 🤭 I stared at her for a second, because I was confused as to why she asked me that as if she thought I was lying or something. I answer her and say yes. She looks at me with an unconvinced face and says, "Ok, I'll be back, hang tight." About 15 minutes go by and she comes back with my 'friend'. She sits us down and tells us that this situation isn't something to play with and tells us she is going to call our parents if we were playing. She then sends my friend back to the room he was in and look at me and says, "Stop lying and please tell me the situation."

😤 At this point I am about to break down because who did I look like to be lying about something like that. I began to cry and tell her through my tears that the situation actually happened and that I wasn't lying. She says ok and calls my mom.

Now, I was starting to get a headache because I was crying so much because I was so mad that she didn't believe me and that my 'friend' denied what he did to me. She hangs up the phone and says, "your parents didn't answer." In that moment I was so frustrated with the whole situation and the fact that my own principal didn't believe that I was touched inappropriately. Whether he did it on purpose or not it didn't matter to me it happened and I knew it was wrong and that some actions needed to be taken. I remember trying so hard to just yell at my principal and say, "How do you not believe me? How could you think I'm lying about something so serious to me?" 😡 I had to realize that she was being ignorant and choosing to believe my 'friend' over the person who actually got sexually assaulted.

I remember getting picked up from school that day and I asked my mom if she had got a call from the principal and she said no. I told her something had happened to me and that I needed to talk to both her and my dad at the same time. So, we got home and waited for my dad to get home from work. Eventually, I told them what happened and got frustrated all over again and cried even more than I did in the principal's office because I had to tell my parents that their child was sexually assaulted at her own elementary school. It was very hard for me to wrap my head around all of it even after telling my parents. 'Til this day it is very hard for me to wrap my head around because I never understood why my 'friend' did what he did and why my principal didn't believe me.

I can say that although I didn't have the worst sexual assault story that you may have ever heard before. It was still sexual assault. I still went through it, unfortunately, but one thing I'm never going to allow that experience to do is scar me and my future. I don't take sexual assault lightly. It is a very, serious thing, no matter how extreme it may be to you. Someone violating someone, whether it was on purpose or not, can be very tormenting and hard for people to get over. You always have to be sensitive because you never know what people have been through or what they are going through. Learning to check the temperature of the people you engage with on a daily basis and being able to know what you should say or ask in that moment, is a very important skill to learn, and it's a skill that I'm personally still learning. When I say check the temperature of the people around you, I mean to analyze the people, but don't assume anything.

This all happened to me in the second grade. Then you know what the crazy part is about seven years later I get a follow request on my Instagram with the exact name of the 'friend' that sexually assaulted me during the whole dice situation. The person who sexually assaulted me followed me on Instagram! Now, there are some people who will say not to follow him back.

Some will say to block him, but you know what I did? I followed him back. Some of y'all are holding grudges because someone did something that the world categories as unforgivable, so you just never let go of the pain, trauma, anger, sadness etc. Little do you know that you are holding on to all those things is causing your sleepless nights, your short temper, your daily anxiety etc. You have to let go and let God.

Know that if you've accepted Jesus Christ as your Lord and Savior, He's got you. 😌👍

If Jesus held grudges, we wouldn't be half the people we are today. Imagine if Jesus said, "Well, he denied me, so I'm not going to talk to him or anyone he's close too?" That would be crazy right? Being a follower of Christ and really knowing God for yourself and having a relationship with him, helps you to learn that what the world does or sees as a solution, God doesn't.

Knowing how to differentiate the two and being able to choose whether to go with what the world says or with what the Word says is something you must learn how to do and be cautious of.

I am still learning that every person that wants to be my friend isn't trying to do something to me that the world sees as unforgivable. I am in this world, but I am not of this world (Romans 12:2). Meaning that, although I was born here and raised here, I will choose to not be conformed to becoming like the world. It's a peregrination that I'm on and it may take a while, but I know the process will be worth the results in the end. Life is crazy, but don't allow your life to make you crazy. 🤗

DELIVERED · 53

> "Our lives begin to end the day we become silent about the things that matter."
>
> - Martin Luther King Jr.

CHAPTER 3

Low Battery - The Pitch-Black Phase

In June of 2017, I went through a suicidal phase. Everything seemingly went downhill for me. It was the year I was getting promoted from eighth grade to start high school. For my entire middle school experience, I was a very, quiet student. I was a heavy observer. I knew everything about what was going on around me, but no one knew what was going on within me at all. I didn't speak much, not even to the people I called my friends. I was a good student. I got good grades and worked hard for what I wanted, but who would have ever thought that I would go through this?

No one would think this about the quiet church girl, the gymnast, the girl who is the middle child of five, the girl who danced in school without being afraid, the girl who was always there for her friends, the girl who stood up for what she believed in no matter how crazy she sounded to others around her. Who would have guessed the girl that grew up on VeggieTales hearing, "God made you special and he loves you very much", would go through something like this? No one would ever guess me. But, let me tell you something, if you are a child of God, living life is automatically going to be hard or challenging because the devil sees you as a threat to his world, so he is going to try everything to take you down. At the time, I didn't really know who I was in the word of God. I knew that I was fearfully and wonderfully made, but I never really knew what that meant for ME. I would hear it in church a lot but could never really define it for myself. I had a relationship with the church building more than the person I went to the building to worship corporately.

My relationship with God wasn't where it should have been in that time of my life, so I began to fall back. School was getting hard, friends started turning on me, and I just felt as if my world was crashing down right in front of me. I began to look for every other way out of my situation other than running to God. I felt as if God wasn't doing anything for me. 😔 Little did I know that him waking me up every day was him working through me. 🤭 I didn't have that understanding at the time, so I didn't know. No one I was close to knew what was going on with me, so they couldn't help me either. I began to feel less than, not worth it and ugly, etc. I was focused so much on people's opinion of me instead of what God said, that I slowly started losing myself.

I remember the weeks it all went down like yesterday. It was the week right before my eight-grade cruise and promotion ceremony. I was stressed because school was coming to an end and my grades weren't where I wanted them to be. I was sad that I would be leaving some of my friends because we were all going to different high schools. My best friend had moved earlier in the year and that was hard for me to deal with because we had planned out what high school we were going to and how much fun we would have together.

This whole suicide phase and thought process was a build-up of emotions that I never let go of. I knew that what I was feeling was of the devil. My parents told me that, but I didn't want to talk to anyone. I felt that if I spoke up about what I was going through no one would believe me and that they would just throw scriptures at me. I always seemed happy and put together. I always seemed like the strong one. A lot of my friends would talk to me about their problems, but they would never ask me about mine, because I always seemed ok. Key word 'seemed'.

I remember my friends calling me the mom of the friend group because I always took care of everyone before myself, and no one knew what I was going through. I thought that this feeling of me wanting to cut my neck open and just letting myself bleed to death would go away. Little did I know that if I didn't handle the root of my issue, then I would always have that issue in my life.

You can't half-do anything in life. If you half-do stuff, you can't be mad when you get half-done results. For example, imagine for a second that you are making cookies for the first time. Instead of looking up a cookie recipe you try to follow what you saw the bakers on a baking show do. Somehow when you are making the cookies you put baking soda in the cookies instead of baking powder. You probably would have made some very disgusting tasting cookies.

Well, you can't cut corners and take shortcuts and expect full results in whatever you are doing. I didn't realize that I was doing half the job, so some days I felt fine and others I didn't. Some days I would talk to God about it and some days I felt that it was unnecessary to talk to Him. It got to the point where my behavior, my choices and my choice of clothing was a reflection of how I was feeling. I began to dress differently. I wore more baggy looking clothes and darker colors. I looked and felt tired all the time.

I wasn't sleeping well because I allowed my thoughts to keep me awake at night. I began to be very disrespectful to my parents, siblings, friends and even my teachers. One thing I've learned while going through this is that I can't live by feelings alone. No one should ever live by feelings alone because a lot of times we may feel like doing something that we shouldn't do. Everything is mental. What we allow in our minds will eventually come out. I thought I wasn't worth it and all this stuff. I thought about it so much that it began to show through in how I dressed and behaved. I had a conversation with the devil almost every day and he was telling me all these negative things and I began to believe everything he told me.

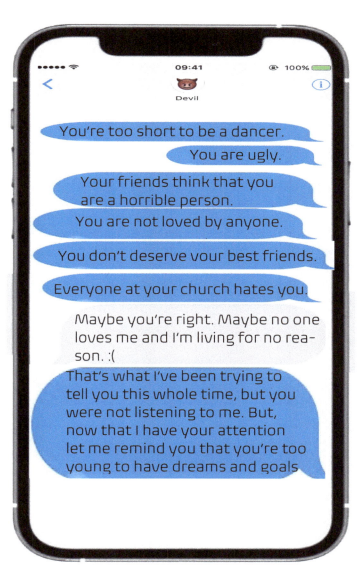

I was so confident in myself that I didn't realize that me entertaining the thoughts, or the "messages" of the devil was getting into my subconscious. I began to allow these thoughts to cloud my mind and I began to second guess if they were actually true.

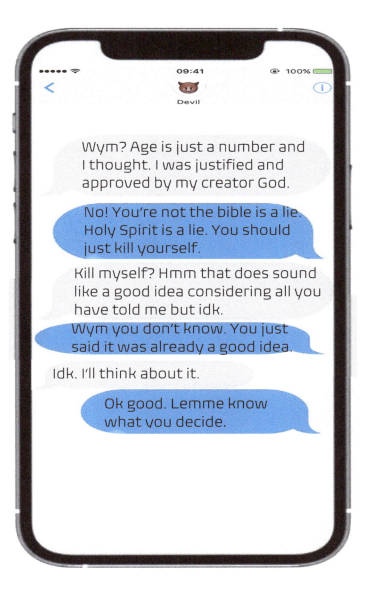

At this point I became less confident in myself. I was slowly allowing myself to think that all these bad things that the devil was telling me in my head were true. My relationship with God became wishy washy. I trusted the devil more than Holy Spirit, and that put me in a really, bad position.

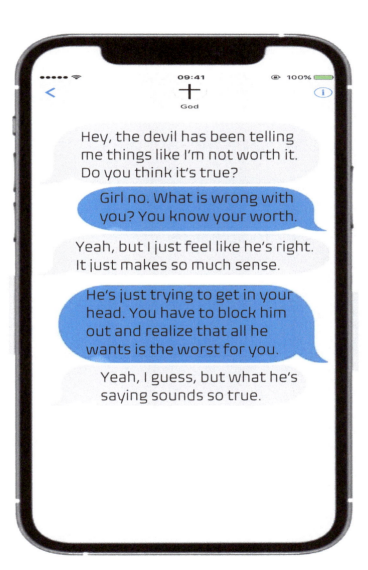

Holy Spirit was trying to tell me that everything that the devil was saying was wrong and that it meant nothing. I became best friends with my flesh to the point where I began to live by my feelings alone because I thought they made more sense than my helper, aka Holy Spirit. I was so small minded that I didn't really believe what the Holy Spirit was telling me.

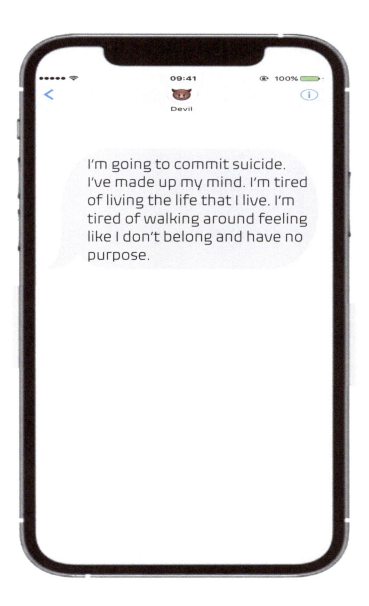

Another school week had started, and it was days before I planned to commit suicide, but I just felt like I couldn't do it. Then, I woke up one morning and went in the shower. After my shower, the mirror in the bathroom was fogged up, so I took my right pointer finger and wrote the words. "I don't want to live anymore. Goodbye family." I went to my room and tried to get ready for school and figure out how I was going to cover up all the redness on my face from crying. My eyes looked like I'd been smoking weed.

As I was getting my bag prepared for school, I heard my oldest sister walk into the bathroom where I wrote on the mirror. She immediately ran out yelling, "Where is Nailah?!" "Nailah!", in a panicking tone. Meanwhile, I am crying so hard in my room I couldn't even see through my tears. My sister comes banging on my door. I didn't answer. She bangs again and at this point my parents and the rest of my siblings are trying to figure out what is going on, while still trying to get ready for school and work. She bangs one more time and I didn't answer once again, so she swings open my room door and gives a huge sigh of relief. She asks me if I wrote those words on the mirror. I look at her with my eyes full of tears and can't even form the word yes in my mouth to be able to answer her. Both my parents run down the steps toward my room and are so confused.

I'm sitting on the ground crying trying to tune out everything that is going on as my sister is telling them what she saw written on the mirror in the bathroom. My parents asked me what's wrong, and I couldn't bring myself to tell the two people who birthed me, the two people who love me even when I do wrong, the two people who have my best interest at heart. I couldn't bring myself to say that I didn't want to live anymore. I thought that if I said something that they would break down right in front of me, because what parent wants to hear their own child say that they don't want to live anymore.

They made the decision to not send me to school that day, so I went to work with my Dad and spent the entire day with him. I didn't speak to him for several hours because I just felt so dead inside. I felt like my voice was taken and I still didn't know what to say so that he didn't break down and cry right in front of me. I didn't want to see or hear his pain after I told him that his daughter didn't want to live anymore.

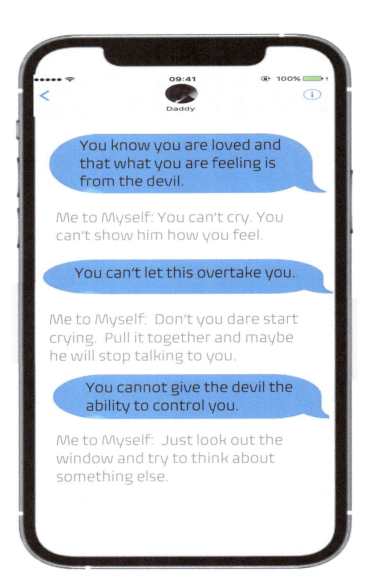

The actual day that I was going to commit suicide, I had just gotten home from school and I had no homework since the school year was coming to a close. At this point, I was fully convinced that I didn't belong on earth and that I had no purpose. I literally felt like a body walking around with no meaning. I had just started to become very close with one of the most amazing human beings I think I've ever met.

For months leading up to this, he would always check on me and make sure that I was good. Little did I know that him checking up on me would become one of the most important things to me 'til this day.

Two weeks before the day of the attempt, I had called him one day and I was so frustrated with myself and my life, but I tried to not let it show in my face. I remember him saying to me, "I know something is going on with you and I can't completely figure it out, but I'm here for you. Please don't shut me out." When he told me that I tried so hard to hold back the tears in my eyes because I knew that if I cried in front of him or looked like I was going to cry in front of him, he would ask me over and over again what was wrong, and he would just stare at me until I told him every little detail, so that he could at least help me in some type of way.

Two days later, I am sitting and crying on the bathroom floor, the same bathroom I had wrote on the mirror, contemplating whether I should go grab the biggest knife from the kitchen and just cut my neck open and wait for my family to find me sitting in my own blood. I was so tired of feeling unwanted and hurt. I just wanted to end all those feelings. I knew that if I killed myself, I would be going to heaven since I accepted Jesus Christ as my Lord and Savior, so I didn't care at all, because I knew that I would be in a better place. I felt as though I had no purpose, so there was no reason for me to be there. After all, I thought, if I killed myself it would be better for everyone close to me, because I thought I was unwanted and that no one understood me.

As I was sitting there, I got a facetime call from the same person who had checked up on me two days before. I turned the camera face down because I didn't want him to see that I was crying and holding a knife. I told him the situation and he says something along the lines of "your life is worth living, the devil is just messing with you. Don't fall into the trap. I'm here for you." Little did I know that call was going to save my life. I have to give him pretty much full credit because if it wasn't for him, I would not be alive right now. If he did not allow God to use him to check on me, I would not have been able to write this book and share this part of my story with the world. JW, my best friend of three years and more to come, is the main person responsible 'til this day for why I am still alive and why I do not take my life and life in general for granted. 🙏

    My parents were trying to encourage me, but I really felt like they didn't understand, and I needed to hear it from someone close to my age. This experience was a huge example of how following God's timing and listening when he speaks can help you in the long run. If he didn't hear God's voice and check on me frequently, if he didn't call me, and if I didn't answer, I can tell you right now that I probably wouldn't still be alive today. As sad as it seems, I wouldn't. We always have to remember that God will put you in people's paths that have your answer or will lead you to your answer. It's all a matter of if you are willing to follow God's instructions and allow him to use you completely. 😊

Having an ear to hear and understand God is something you should prioritize having. Being in the right place at the right time is very important. Someone is counting on you to do what you're supposed to do. The decisions you make can potentially have the power of giving life to someone you may know or someone you may not know. Don't hold in how you feel because you are afraid of how people will react. Your feelings are valid. Don't be crazy and not get help. It is a hard process to go through but trust me when I say that life is worth living 🥹, no matter how many obstacles get thrown at you, no matter how hard it may seem. You have a life to live and a purpose to fulfill.

DELIVERED · 97

"What really matters is not whether we have problems, but how we go through them. We must keep going on to make it through whatever we are facing."

- Rosa Parks

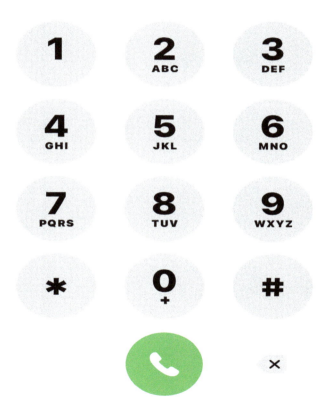

CHAPTER 4

Everyone's Fav 6-letter word...School

Ahh yesss, school... That place that they say we must go to be successful. They say if you want a better chance at life, then go to school. Who are 'they' anyway and why are we so concerned about what 'they' say...LOL😂? I have a love-hate relationship with school. I am a pretty, smart person, but I've come to the conclusion that school isn't for me…LOL. I have always been the person that my classmates run to for the answers, but school is just not for me. First off, people can be very weird, and you can learn a lot about people when you go through a few years of school with them. I look at school as an opportunity to grow, but I know that it's not the only way I can grow and obtain information from an educational standpoint. School is like that one family member's house that you don't really want to go to, but you know if you go you will see your favorite cousin. Like, it's that place that we dread going to sometimes, but also that place that we go to because we don't want to be stuck at home.

School was very hard for me when I was younger. Even now that I'm in high school, it's been a little bit harder, but I've always put myself in a position to challenge myself and understand that if I don't pass this one test, I'm still OK. But, one thing I suggest is to never let yourself get too comfortable with not passing, because then you gradually become so numb to grades that you do nothing. I've had multiple experiences at school from elementary through high school where I just felt that school was way too hard for me, and then I didn't even care to understand, which led to the point of me not performing my best in school. It was one of the worst decisions I've made as a student.

I got so comfortable with where I was at as it related to my grades that I felt like I couldn't deal with school anymore. I felt that I would never understand school or what my teachers were trying to teach me. I felt that nobody could teach me how I needed to be taught in order for me to fully understand each and every concept that was presented to me.

Since I became comfortable and disgustedly okay with the fact that I thought I wasn't teachable, my grades dropped dramatically, then my GPA dropped, and everything school-wise just went downhill for me. It caused me a lot of stress because I didn't know how to get my grades up and I didn't know how to explain to my parents, who strongly believe in education, that I thought school was just not for me.

Now that I've looked back on that moment, I see that it was all just pure laziness and me being small-minded and not open to other options that had the potential of helping me a lot. Me telling myself that I couldn't do it and that school was too hard, knowing that I was more than capable of doing it and maintaining the grades that I wanted, wasn't helping my situation.

School can be as hard as you make it or as easy as you're willing to make it. You have to choose to change and 'faith it' 'til you make it, if you have too.

If you want something, make a plan, write it out and stick to it. I wanted straight A's, so I told myself constantly that I was going to get straight A's. I reminded myself that if I got a low grade on a test that I couldn't retake, I would need to work a little bit harder to recover from it. Habakkuk 2:2

says, "Write the vision, make it plain". If you have a vision of getting straight A's or getting on honor roll or getting maybe only getting two C's on your report card, you have to write that down. You have to have a plan or else you're just gonna have that in your head, and maybe you said it a couple times out into the atmosphere so it can manifest, but you need a plan so that you can accomplish your goal. You can't just want it to manifest and have no plan of action.

    I remember when I was in second grade and that was when everything was supposedly easy as a student, but to me one of the hardest things for me was reading and comprehension. I look back at my struggles now and I still can't figure out why it was so hard for me to read and comprehend…LOL.

In my second-grade class, we used to have sections of the day when we had to read books and we had to take a reading test to figure out what our Lexile score was and how we could increase it. We would go to the library every week and we were able to check out at least two books. I would always pick out, you know, the gymnastics book, the Dr. Seuss books, the fairy books or the Magic Tree House books, nothing challenging, just something entertaining.

What I didn't realize was that me going for the easy stuff was making it even harder for me to pick up a book that was higher than my reading level. I put myself in a bad position reading-wise because I wanted something easy.

I remember my teacher having to send me home with books to help me better understand how to read and comprehend. I used to have more homework than everybody else in my class because I was falling behind in reading in the second grade. I felt so dumb. I felt stupid. I felt as if I couldn't do it and I never told myself that I could until later on.

Throughout the year I realized that I didn't want those books anymore. I didn't want to get sent home with books. So, I had to do something about it. I told myself I'm no longer going to be sent home with books, so I made a plan to read at least one book every couple weeks. I made myself a plan that I would read everything I picked up in my kitchen and everything I saw on TV. I would read so that my comprehension and my reading skills would increase for the better.

When you tell yourself that you can't complete a task or that you don't have the capacity to do something, it becomes a constant battle between you and your mind, because all of those thoughts are now in your subconscious. What you should do is constantly remind yourself that you are more than capable of completing anything you put your mind to.

> *Yet in all these things we are more than conquerors through Him who loved us.*
>
> *~ Romans 8:37 NKJV*

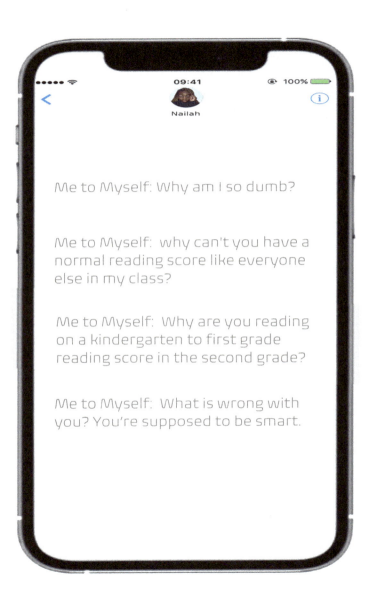

In my freshman year of high school, I joined the dance team. I have always loved dance 💃. Dance has helped me through a lot of my life's roller coasters because it's given me the opportunity to express how I was feeling through movement instead of words, which was really big for me. Anyway, that is not what we are talking about right now...LOL. I joined the dance team, and everything was going great until about the end of the second quarter. School was just getting a little too hard for me. I took on too much at once, which I thought I could handle at the time. Eventually, my parents said that it was a good idea to not continue on the dance team for the winter season. Of course, I was kind of mad because I love dance, so it was hard for me to not to be a part of the dance team for the second part of the school year. I had to remember that my parents had my best interest in mind, and I knew my grades weren't where they could have been. I was getting C's and D's and I am an A's and B's student, so that wasn't cutting it. You should listen to your parents no matter what age you are. Yes, they can be annoying sometimes, but you are also annoying to them sometimes...LOL 😳. They just want the best for you, and you should too.

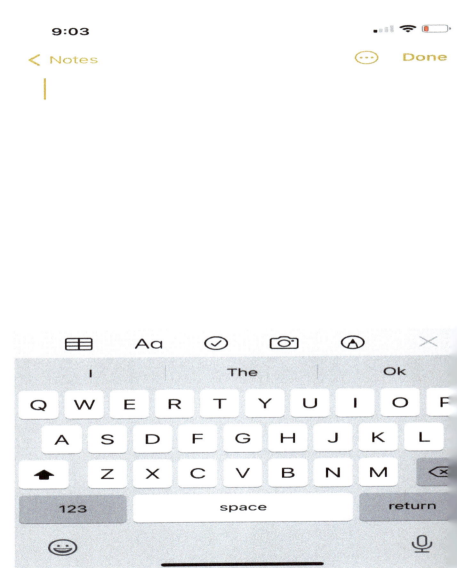

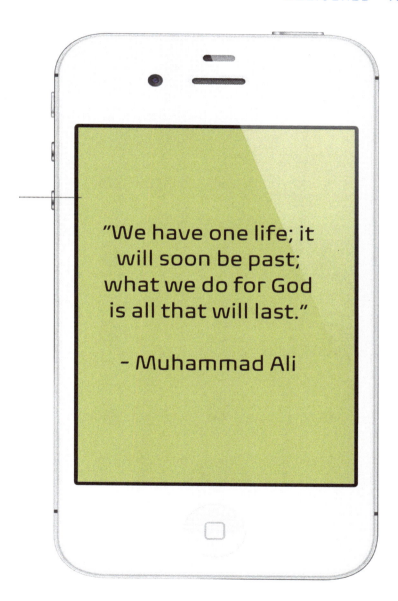

CHAPTER 5

#NoCap - Relationships

Now me personally, I don't choose my friends based on personality or status. I choose my friends off of mindset and maturity. There was a time when I was younger, when I wanted to be a part of the 'in' crowd. I wanted all the tea about other friend groups just because I thought it would be interesting. I was simply immature. I was too young to understand that those people just wanted to be seen and that they had nothing to offer me to make me a better person. If you are friends or acquaintances with people who are pulling you down, then why are you friends with them? That is so pointless. 🙄 If you are trying to go up why are you conversing with someone who wants to go down? 🤪 I know the saying "choose your friends wisely" is a very, popular phrase, but it's also a very accurate phrase. I can't begin to tell you how many times I thought I was friends with a certain type of person and then weeks, months or years down the road I found out stuff about them that I didn't like. Sooner or later, if you keep hanging out or talking to people that have qualities you don't like, you will pick up those same qualities without even realizing it. Not to say you have to be friends with people who are "perfect", because at the end of the day no one is perfect. Just don't be stuck in a friendship with someone with the mindset of negativity, who rejects personal growth.

After choosing those relationships, make sure you stand your ground. What I mean by that is, make sure you remain YOU!! Don't become the other person or people that you have a relationship with. You both or you all should be bringing something to the table. You should be checking one another. When someone you have a relationship with is out of line, you shouldn't allow them to just stay out of line, you should talk to them about it. After you talk to them about it, the rest is up to them. Whether or not they use what you said is now in their control. You've done your part. Now, it's time for them to do there's.

There was this one time in seventh grade when I was really close to this group of girls. One week the girls in the group began to talk about another one of the girls that I was really, really close to at the time. She had told me the problem and I was mad because it was stupid, and then the fact that they called each other friends and started talking about one another was disgusting to me. This back and forth went on for a little while and was starting to affect our entire friend group. Everyone else in the group started choosing sides, including me.

I was so mad that one afternoon after school I was at my house and I was texting my friend that I was really close to and she was asking me what she should do. I told her I would talk to the other girl. Now, if you know me personally, I'm a very blunt, straight to the point kind of person, and having that quality has helped me a lot, but has also gotten me in trouble a lot. I care about people's feelings, but I also knew that when I was right, I was going to say it like it was, and I could care less what happened afterwards.

So, my friend and I are texting, and before I could even finish texting her, I start texting the other girl and I tell the girl to basically shut her mouth because she was really trying to talk about my friend. The funny thing was that our teacher knew the situation and was telling us to stop talking about each other because nothing was getting resolved, and we were losing friends over a petty situation. So, I tell the girl that we literally just talked about this issue with our teacher. One thing about me is that I will go to war for my friends and the people I care about, no matter the cost, so when she told me to shut up and stop texting her, it didn't sit well with me at all. I told her that literally the whole school knew the situation because she was running her mouth too much and that she wouldn't have any friends going into eighth grade because she was being very petty to someone she called a friend. She had told me that basically I didn't know the whole story, so I had no right to speak on it, and it's not my place to speak for my friend.

In the end, I actually got called down to see the principal with her, and the principal threatened to call my parents, and told me that when I was texting the girl the day before police were monitoring her account, so they saw everything I said. I just sat there in awe because it's like she went to the extreme for something really petty, and I got in trouble for trying to help my friend. I didn't understand at the time, but I really just needed to stay in my lane and keep quiet because like she said, it wasn't my place to speak on something I had little to no knowledge about. I could've approached the whole situation differently, but I would never apologize for standing up for my friend.

Long story short my parents were never called the girl and I forgave each other, and we laughed about it and became friends, and everything was pretty much cool after that. My point of saying all this is to choose your friends wisely, and don't be blind to the truth, because I was and that got me nowhere. The truth was, before I even stepped to the girl, the problem was already resolved, and I was just blowing it all out of proportion. Anyway, that was my little rant/advice about relationships. Just pay attention and choose your friends wisely, because everyone that claims to be your friend may just want to learn all of your blind spots, so that they can try to take you down.

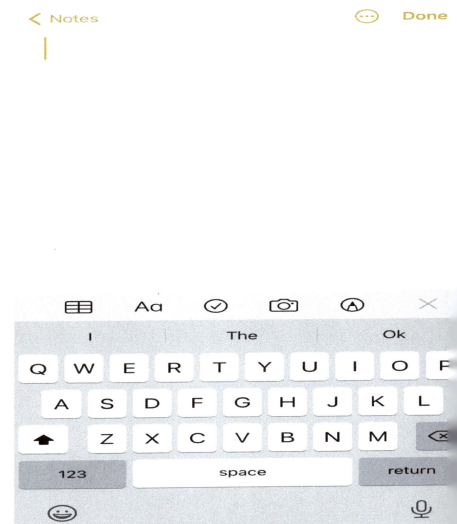

"The chances you take, the people you meet, the people you love, the faith that you have. That's what's going to define you."

- Denzel Washington

6

Add Number

1	**2** ABC	**3** DEF
4 GHI	**5** JKL	**6** MNO
7 PQRS	**8** TUV	**9** WXYZ
✱	**0** +	#

CHAPTER 6

No Filter – Insecurities & Self-Confidence

Hmm... the word insecurities. The word that's used when you stand in front of a mirror for over an hour trying to figure out if the dress your mom bought you is going to show all of your "problem areas". It is this mindset that we as people take on sometimes and tell ourselves it's ok to not think that we are beautiful, or it's ok to not think we are handsome, but that's not true. Everyone has this way of controlling their mind, but sometimes we put our minds on autopilot and expect not to feel some type of way when the turbulence hits.

We are scrolling on Instagram and we see a girl with a nice body and nice thick eyebrows. We expect that what we put in our subconscious will not affect the way we think, move, and speak. We think that we are unaffected by what we see on our timelines and what we crave to look like will just go away. Huh, that's funny. We put ourselves in this box, thinking that if I don't have the freshest hairline with the wavest waves (and yes, I just made up the word wavest and what about it lol) I will never be beautiful or handsome in my own eyes or the eyes of others.

Social media is the jail cell of small-minded people. Social media isn't and should never become your reality, because at the end of the day, when all technology is off and you are alone in your room, it's just you and your almost six pack abs, you and your hair as long as Rapunzel's, you and you stretch marks that are wrapped around your body as decoration, you and you big forehead, you and you chocolatey skin, you and your very squinty eyes, you and your skinny, but beautiful body, you and your 30 by 30 jeans, you and your sculpted body, you and your 4'6-5'0 self, you and your big nose, you and your...

At the end of the day, it's JUST YOU, beautifully made in the image of God, that you are ashamed of because of what? The standard? The standard is Genesis 1:27 and Psalms 139:14. You are fearfully and wonderfully made in the image of God. Inside and out. Body and Soul. Heart and Mind.

You are marvelously made! Learning that for yourself and knowing that for yourself is a journey you have to take to know that you are all that and a bag of chips.

Confidence isn't something you just wake up with. You must choose confidence just like you choose happiness. You have to wake up every day, look in the mirror and tell yourself that you are smart, you are beautiful, you are talented, you are special, you got bodyyy, you are clean with or without a haircut. You have to love your natural stage self, that wake up in the morning with a durag or a bonnet stage self. That I didn't work out yesterday, but that's ok self. LOVE YOURSELF 💞. You didn't come out the womb with the extra, so that's a prime example that you don't need the extra.

Being confident in your own skin and loving yourself is very important. Knowing that you may not be the best version of yourself yet, but still loving yourself through the process is essential. Although it's not easy, it will be one of the best things you choose to do in your life.

We love because He first loved us.
~ 1 John 4:19 ESV

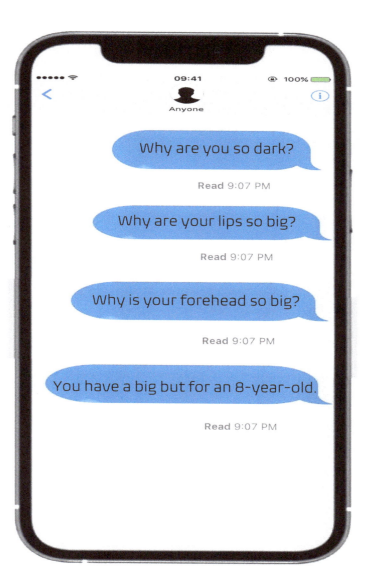

As a child I was always told that my lips were huge and that my forehead was even bigger. I didn't know what to think because at the time I didn't have the best relationship with my creator, God. I thought that what people told me almost every day in school was true. I was also told I was too dark. I never knew that there could be too dark because there isn't such a thing as too dark or too light. I was young and I was being manipulated by the thoughts and opinions of people I didn't even know and people I was extremely close to. I was also constantly told that I was beautiful for a black girl. Like what does that even mean? I was told contradicting statements that I eventually began to believe because I didn't know anything else. It felt as if almost everyday someone had something to say about me. I began to become insecure about it.

In July of 2020 I was going through a phase where I didn't really like my body. Since we were in quarantine, while everyone else was eating more and gaining weight, I actually ate less than I did when life was "normal" and lost weight. No, my parents didn't starve me. This was a habit that I fell into because I would do so much during the day that I would literally delay eating. I also got tired of eating the same food, although it was healthy.

When I was at school, I always had snacks in my backpack and I always had friends who would give me snacks in my classes. I am currently vegan. I have been for a number of years. Now that we were home all day, we ate even healthier, so losing weight was easier.

That habit of me eating less eventually changed how I viewed myself every time I looked in the mirror. I disliked my body because I was losing weight. I remember throughout middle school and my freshman and sophomore year of high school people would tell me that my body was goals and all this stuff. I struggled to see what they were seeing in me. It was so mentally and physically draining.

I think because of the constant swiping on social media, I became manipulated into thinking that I had to look a certain way in order to love myself and be categorized as beautiful. Society, social media, people etc., no one can tell me that I'm beautiful because of this or that. In reality, we are all beautiful or handsome, but knowing that for yourself is when you really start to believe that you are, without even having to looking in a mirror or without people having to tell you that you are. It's a process, especially if you've been insecure about yourself for a long period of time; but a period can last as long as you want it to. If you want to change how you view yourself as a person, you must first change your mindset about yourself.

    The devil will try anything to get into your head because before that time I was never insecure. People tried to make me feel insecure about how big my lips and my forehead were, but I was never insecure. 👩🏽‍🦱 I have always been very confident in myself as a person. I always saw my flaws as a beauty mark of something I could use to grow. Being flawed is being human. It's natural to be flawed and to not understand why you are flawed, but what you should never do is tell yourself that you aren't enough because you have flaws. Everyone has flaws and whether you let it ruin you or not is a decision you constantly have to make for yourself. You can't tell yourself that just because you are on the bigger side doesn't mean you can't dance. You can't tell yourself that just because you're on the shorter side you can't play basketball.

You know what's crazy though, when I was younger people used to hate on me for my lips, butt and curves, but now it's like everyone wants what I have naturally. Now, this isn't intended to shoot people down or make them feel less than, it's just an interesting observation to me. I'm not saying don't get your body done or don't fix what you don't like but understand that you are beautiful/handsome without all of that, and please, please, please don't do it because you want to fit into the trend of society, because you want a body like Nicki Minaj at the age of 15. God made you the way you are for a reason. Learn it, love it and be ok with it. Periodt 😌

> *I will praise You, for I am fearfully and wonderfully made;*
>
> *~ Psalm 139:14a NKJV*

> "People don't want to experience change; they just want to wake up, and it's different."
>
> – Chadwick Boseman

7

Add Number

1	2 ABC	3 DEF
4 GHI	5 JKL	6 MNO
7 PQRS	8 TUV	9 WXYZ
*	0 +	#

Favorites Recents Contacts **Keypad** Voicemail

CHAPTER 7

My Messages - DELIVERED

Whew... I know that was a lot. All of that in 16 years. Crazy right! I think I can classify myself as a living, walking, talking, moving, breathing miracle after all of that LOL. One thing that I can say I've learned personally from experiencing all of this is that my mindset is wise beyond my years, but that doesn't mean that there isn't more to learn. I also learned that I didn't have to go through any of that to learn what I did, but the reality is that I did go through all of that, and I came out on top. Your life can be as crazy as you allow it to be. Live, breathe, laugh, and cry because you are living a life full of endless battles to be won. Life is this precious thing that we all have, so never take your life or another person's life for granted. Someone died so you could live. Make your decisions in life wisely. Don't be dumb with your life. 🤪 Know that someone is going to hate on you because you have something that they don't. Don't even concern yourself with haters because they are irrelevant. Know that you will have haters, but that you will also have so many other people who will love you for you 😍.

Make sure you have someone in your corner telling you what you need to hear opposed to what you want to hear. The truth is the truth, and you can't change it or rearrange it to try to make it fit the truth you want to hear. If you didn't take away anything from all of that. Take away the fact that you are more than capable to change any situation you end up in, if you are willing to change your mindset. The mind is a powerful thing, but never let that be the only powerful thing that possesses you. After all, it's your mind, so you have full control of it. Never hide from the world just because you are afraid or uncomfortable. Conquer the world. Conquer your situations. Never try to be someone else's definition of perfect. Just be real. Just be you. Always know that God wants to lead and guide you, but you must be willing to give him the steering wheel and just become the passenger in your own life story.

Never underestimate the power that you hold inside of you. I wrote this book based on topics from my journal that I wrote about a lot. The crazy thing is that I'm still not passionate about reading books LOL. It's crazy how God will use something you think has no meaning and turn it into something that does. You have to know that your story matters. Now, I'm not saying to go and write a book, but know that you have something special. My story will always have some meaning in my life, and it will always be a stepping-stone for me in this journey called life.

You must be willing to take a risk and go into the deep end. Stop getting comfortable in the shallow end. The shallow only provides comfortability, not risk, not growth. I'm not talking about a pool, literally. I'm talking about how you know you want to sing more, but you over there scrolling on Instagram watching other people's covers, when people could be watching your own covers. I'm talking about you starting to read books instead of just saying you want to grow your vocabulary. You must be willing to take a step further and go after what you want, and that sometimes means you have to take a dip in the deep end. Be a risk taker and I guarantee that you'll end up in a position that you love. I also want to urge you to fall in love with your passion. I didn't mention it much in this book, but your passion will take you further than you may think. Whether that's acting, singing, producing, drawing, writing, modeling, athletics, etc. Whatever it is, make sure you get clarity from God that it's the thing you are supposed to go after.

Everything that was supposed to kill me physically, mentally, and emotionally I overcame 💪🏾 because I was willing to take a risk and tell myself enough is enough. I didn't want to live a life of misery. Because of that, I live a life where I am grateful every time my feet hit the floor in the morning, because I know what it was like to not want to even get out of bed. Be so in love with your relationship with God, yourself, and your life that you are super excited about waking up every morning. Now, it's not going to be easy, but it's going to be completely worth it. Last thing I'll say is my favorite quote and my favorite scripture.

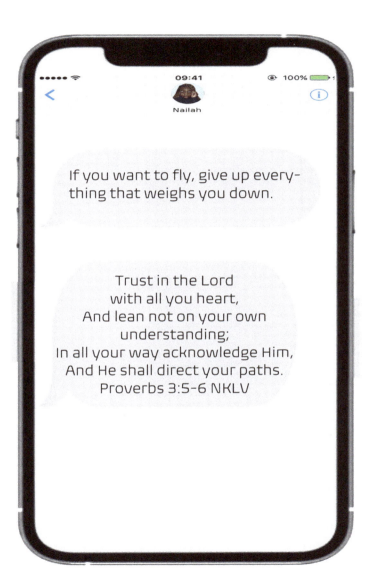

If you want to fly, give up everything that weighs you down.

Trust in the Lord
with all you heart,
And lean not on your own
understanding;
In all your way acknowledge Him,
And He shall direct your paths.
Proverbs 3:5-6 NKLV

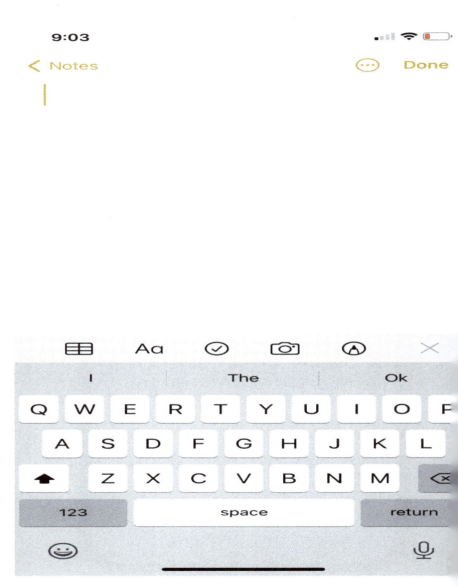

Epilogue
(for any evil thoughts):

So, for years she suffered from multiple evil thoughts. She struggled so much she almost killed herself with them. After a long couple of years of unwanted actions, thoughts, and experiences, she decided to pass away. The 'she' that passed away is all the evil. She was Delivered from everything that she thought had the potential to kill her.

CALL JESUS

Hey, so I found it very necessary to add this to my book because building a relationship with Jesus Christ himself is very important. And, knowing whether you are going to heaven or hell is also VERY important, especially now since we are in the last days. So, if you would like to receive Jesus Christ as your Lord and Savior read this out loud and mean it:

"Father, I ask you to come into my life right now. I confess with my mouth and believe in my heart that you are Lord and that you have been risen from the dead and because of that I am saved."

DELIVERED LIST

I'll start....
1. Anxiety
2. Depression
3. Suicide

Now make your own list:
1.

2.

3.

RESOURCES

National Suicide Prevention Lifeline Number:
800-273-8255

National Sexual Assault Hotline Number:
1-800-656-4673

I would love to hear from you!

Feel free to email me your testimonies, comments and questions at:

Deliveredbook@gmail.com

Make sure to follow me at

@flyy_nai

And follow my talk page, where I start conversations that need
to be discussed, and you can hear how I feel about different topics,
large and small.

@wordsbynaii

Lightning Source UK Ltd.
Milton Keynes UK
UKHW051047270223
417719UK00011B/145